FIERCE: Fearless Women of the Bible

CRYSTAL JONES

ISBN: 193686732X
ISBN-13: 9781936867325

DEDICATION

I would like to dedicate this book to all of my beautiful nieces:

Aries Winans, Tamika Miller, LaToya Brown, Cierra Walker, Taneshia Underwood, Aiesha James, Asia Thomas, Dasia Ingram, India Thomas, Mariah Walker, Jordan Owens, Tabitha West, Ryan Walker, DeNaja Allen, Pier Walker, Shebrie Harris, Victoria Jones, Angela Harris, and Ashley Harris

May you grow fierce and fearless. Don't let anything hinder you from the adventure you are called to live. Don't settle for less than God's absolute best. Do the things that scare you. Take risks. Be all that you can possibly be. Know this, in order to soar, you must first leap. Above everything else, trust God. I love you, but He loves you more.

CONTENTS

ACKNOWLEDGMENTS

I am always thankful to my Loving and Faithful Lord for every opportunity He offers me to speak to His people. He is the Lion of Judah, fierce and fearless and all the things that I want to be. Thank you, Jesus for trusting me with your word! I don't take what you give me for granted. I love you and honor you always.

I also acknowledge the alpha leader of my pride, my roaring and loving husband, Apostle Oscar Jones. I love you and appreciate you always seeing so much more in me than I was able to see in myself. You are such an outstanding man of God. It is my honor to follow your lead.

1
WONDER WOMEN

Wonder women are those women who stand out as super-heroine types. These ladies are not clothed in capes and costumes, but in faith. They are women who trust God in spite of the obstacles they face. They defy religion and break the rules. Wonder women impact history and change the world. Such are the women who are portrayed in these pages.

The women of the Old and New Testaments faced many challenges in their time and culture, often viewed as second class citizens. They were unable to own possessions or property. Oppressed, rejected and disregarded, they had to stand strong in their femininity. Men often tried to strip them of their authority, their spirituality, and their voice. They were restricted in many ways.

This was never the intention of our Loving Lord. He created woman to be free. She was created to be a leader in God's Kingdom. He empowered her and charged her to bring forth life and crush the head of the enemy. In God's mind, women would be fierce and powerful, as she possessed His very nature. Just like man, she was created in

God's image. So her capacity is far reaching. In God's mind, the man and woman would operate as a team! This dynamic duo would be a force to be reckoned with.

So to see many of these women rise to their occasions in spite of their challenges is nothing short of astonishing. They went to war, defended their families, sacrificed their pleasures, moved to foreign countries and fought for what belonged to them as people of God. They laid it all out on the line, as if they had nothing to lose.

Everything was against them: the customs, the laws, and even (at times) their men. Nevertheless they stood in faith, knowing that God would back them up. Some of them named and some unnamed. But all equally amazing. They were not perfect women, but holy women.

There is something most wonder-ful about being female. Woman is a beautiful and delicate creature with a quiet strength – until it is unveiled. Much like the animal that keeps to herself until her cubs are at risk. She rises up. She roars. And you had better listen. Because she is fierce and provocative. Her strength under pressure is like a volcano. She will erupt and deal harshly with the enemy. At the same time, she is compassionate and nurturing and will stroke the head of one in need as he lay upon her chest. We are complex beings indeed.

Certainly there are far more fierce women than the few I have highlighted in this book. These are the Fabulous 14. Read their stories. Understand their triumphs. Feel their brokenness. Find the point of relativity. Their stories are our stories. They were chosen because of the way they demonstrated fearlessness with limited power and resources. They felt compelled to be different. They didn't want to just fall in line and be invisible. These fabulous women broke through and broke out. They did it out of necessity. They did it out of faith. Let their stories change yours.

You, too, are called to be a wonder woman; a woman whose actions cause others to stand in awe of her God. Let your life point to Him. You were born to be fierce.

The word fierce means to be feisty, passionate, and strong. The Fierce Woman speaks the mind of God. She stands up to authority when authority is wrong, she does the right thing regardless of what law or conventional wisdom says. She acts counterculture.

She is a lioness at heart. She has the same protective instinct that the feline has for her cubs. She roars and others back down. She oversees the marginalized. She steps in to protect those who cannot protect themselves, and care for those in need of care.

It is my earnest desire that you might unlock the Fierce Princess Warrior within. And release her to pursue her own adventure. My dear sisters, be all that you can possibly be:

Fearless
Intercessor
Exceptional Leader
Righteous in spirit
Cunning
Empathetic

At the end of each chapter, there is the <u>Becoming A Fierce Woman</u> section. The questions are there to provoke you to think and challenge yourself to grow and to love the skin you are in. Take time to answer each one. Be prayerful and challenge yourself to grow.

CRYSTAL JONES

2
BEAUTY & THE BEAST
FEARLESS ABIGAIL

I Samuel 25:1-42

The Bible describes Abigail as beautiful. While we do not know the details of her outward beauty, her lavish internal beauty spills out on the pages. She is a defender and advocate for those whom she feels responsible. She is described as a woman of understanding.

This Beauty had married a Beast. Nabal was a fool, as the Bible called him. Her marriage had been unpleasant at best. This harsh, rude, godless man continued to get their family into trouble. But even in that, Abigail did not seek to abandon him. She was a loyal wife, a beautiful woman who loved her God. She kept her vow, no matter how difficult Nabal made it for her.

Abigail had a reputation for being wise. One of the servants approached her and asked her to intervene to avert impending disaster. Yes, Nabal had done it again! This time he had disrespected David, the future king of Israel. David was an outlaw, at this time. King Saul's jealousy had set him in pursuit of David. He felt that David was a threat to His throne. However David in his kindness, had taken care of Nabal's herdsmen. Having a need, he sent a request asking for Nabal's help. True to his character, Nabal spurned David. David's emotions clouded his view. And now David and his army were heading to exact revenge upon Nabal and his entire household.

Abigail had been summoned to clean up Nabal's mess. So she donned her cape. I mean, her courage and took food to David and his crew. She pleaded for the life of her obstinate, drunkard of a husband. She humbled herself and reminded David of God's Word and his destiny. She prophesied to him about his future. She was able to calm the future king. He accepted her offering.

It's interesting that she says to David, "May your enemies be as Nabal." As if she knows that Nabal is going to die. The tagline to her dissertation was "Remember me when you come into your kingdom". I believe the Lord had already showed this prophetess the things that were to come concerning her husband.

Being the wise woman that she was, she didn't mention anything to Nabal regarding the threat he brought upon their house until he was sober. When she told him what happened, Nabal was so fearful that he had a stroke and 10 days later, the beast died. The Lord avenged this Beauty and the king came for her hand in marriage.

Some squawk at Abigail's approach and say that she was out of order and not truly submitted to her husband. She defied him and gave to David what Nabal said he couldn't have. I see her as the Bible calls her – wise. She saved Nabal's life. He actually lived about 2 weeks longer than he would have, if Abigail had not acted. There is no honor in sitting still and doing nothing when you know that death is coming to your house. In fact, it would have been shameful. She stood as intercessor on behalf of her husband and her household. She took a risk because it was dangerous for her to approach David in his anger. But she did it anyway. She was prepared to accept whatever the consequences would be.

Nabal didn't deserve her courage and devotion. However she had committed to be the best wife that she could be to him when she covenanted to be a daughter of God. A lesser wife would have stood back and let David do what he was going to do. Or maybe just plead for the lives of herself and her servants and let the chips fall where they may. He would have gotten what was due him, and she could be free of his foolishness. But she didn't.

Abigail rendered the most holy response – she was a fearless intercessor. Albeit she should not have called him a fool. She treated Nabal like he was worthy of her love. What a beautiful spirit Abigail demonstrates! She gave her husband the best part of herself, even when he didn't give her the same.

Some women are 21st Century Beauties living with a Beast. Wisdom demands that these precious daughters, intercede for their husbands, love them and pray for them. The wise will entreat them with kindness, praying for deliverance. Beauties don't forget their covenant. And God doesn't forget them.

Maybe you aren't married to a foolish man. But perhaps your husband behaves in a foolish manner, at times. The wisdom still applies. Love him, support him, intercede for him. God will deliver you. Trust in God and lean on His Word.

Because David acted with wisdom and humility, in responding to Abigail's appeal, God gifted her to him, as his wife, after the demise of Nabal. Surely David found a good thing. May we, as wives, be as beautiful as Abigail.

BECOMING A FIERCE WOMAN

Have you ever found yourself in a precarious situation where your husband put you or your family at risk (financially or otherwise)? How did you handle it?

_____
_____
_____
_____

How should you have handled it?

_____
_____
_____
_____

If you are not married, do you think you could have handled it with the class that Abigail did?　　　Y　　N

Do you consider Abigail to be submitted?
　　　　　　Y　　N
Why/Why Not?

_____
_____
_____

What about Abigail's story stands out to you?

_____
_____
_____
_____

3
A DOG WITH A BONE: CANAANITE WOMAN

———◆———

Matthew 15:21-28

Peeking into a conversation, we get to see the outstanding faith of this Canaanite woman. Jesus had just come to Tyre and Sidon. He came there specifically to meet with her. He didn't happen upon this place. Even though she was not an Israelite, Jesus especially came for her. This nameless woman was from this region. As soon as his conversation with her ends, He exits. He's on to His next encounter.

What was this conversation about? She had a need. She had heard about all that Jesus had done and she believed Him to be who He said He was. She was convinced that He alone held deliverance in His Hand. There were many of his own people who did not believe, but this woman did.

She approaches him with, "Lord, have mercy on me." She doesn't ask for mercy for her daughter, but for herself. She owns the trouble that has found its way into her house. Her daughter was grievously vexed with a devil. Deliverance for her daughter depended on God having

11

mercy on her. She didn't deserve what she was about to ask. But she would ask it nonetheless. If she was going to receive the gift, she knew He was her only resort.

But he seemed to ignore her. We know that is not the intent of such a Gentle God; especially because he had come to the city just to meet with her. It seems to be a testing of her faith. She accepts the challenge. She continues her pleading. The disciples urge him to send her away. That does not deter her. At this point, she falls to her knees. "Lord, help me!" With every slight, she offers a rebuttal. This desperate woman is persistent. She has come for her daughter to be delivered from demons and she is not leaving without it. She stands with bulldog tenacity

Jesus does not send her away at the disciples request. He seems to be prodding her, "How far will you go? How bad do you want it?" He is stirring up her faith.

"I was sent only to the lost sheep of Israel" He says. "It is not right to take the children's bread and toss it to the dogs". At this point, it sounds like Jesus is insulting her. On the contrary, He is emphasizing that his mission is to the Jews first. She must understand and acknowledge this God of the Jews was truly God, unlike any of the many gods of her people. Then she could have access to the deliverance she was requesting.

She was not swayed by this. She responds in kind, "Truth, Lord, but even the dogs eat the crumbs from the master's table". This statement was acknowledgment of His deity and his mission to Israel first. "I'll take whatever is left", she seems to plead.

Jesus is pleased with this fearless daughter. He says to her "You have great faith!" And her daughter was healed at that moment. Her miracle had been granted.

The Lord had every intention of healing her daughter. He had come to the city for this very purpose. But the

Canaanite woman's faith had to be both decreed and demonstrated.

What about us? Are we as humble as the Canaanite woman? Or do we get angry with God when things don't go the way that we think they should? Are we as persistent as she was? Or do we give up petitioning God for what we need?

The Lord has come to deliver the promise to us. But He is only moved by faith. Without it, God is not pleased. Ensure that your faith is passionate and fierce. Stand on what God is able to do. And don't be moved.

BECOMING A FIERCE WOMAN

What has happened in your life where you really needed God to show up?

_____
_____
_____
_____

Did you give up?　　Yes　　No

How did it turn out?

_____
_____
_____
_____

How would you handle that situation differently today?

_____
_____
_____
_____

What about the Caananite woman's story stands out to you?

_____
_____
_____
_____
_____

4
THE LION QUEEN:
DEBORAH

Judges 4

Israel played this game of see-saw with sin. Up and down, back and forth, in and out. God would deliver them and give them peace and they would do evil again. And find themselves at the mercy of their enemies. The people suffered for their own apostasy. And so it was here in the book of Judges, chapter 4. Ehud had delivered them, but now he was dead and God had allowed them to be sold into captivity to the Canaanites. They were being treated cruelly by Jabin, the king; and so they once again cried out to God.

The Lord had already positioned his daughter in place. She completely trusted him. She would bring the word of deliverance to Israel. This trailblazer was born to lead. God had called her as a prophetess and judge over his people. Never before had women been thought to be capable of leading. Women were secondary citizens in both the Israelite and Canaanite cultures. But Deborah arose as a mother in Israel. She gave council and spoke God's truth to His people. And they listened to her, respected her, and knew that it was God speaking through her. They didn't question her leadership. They simply followed her instructions.

The nurturing and wise words of Deborah nudged them back in the place of submission to their God.

She gives the word of the Lord to Barak, that he is to go to battle. Barak backs up. He is not willing to go without her. This was odd. Women did not go with men to battle. The word God gave her to give Barak was that he should take 10,000 men. The Lord never said anything about women. Nevertheless she agreed to accompany Barak. Even though she would be doing something no other woman had done, she was willing. "God will then give the victory into the hand of a woman", she told Barak. And Barak led Israel into war with 10,000 men and 1 woman.

Of course, she was no ordinary woman. She was the valiant woman who could hear from God. Deborah had set a precedent. This leading lady was ready to fight simply because Israel had a word from God.

Yes, she was prophetess, judge, and leader, but she was not who God originally chose to go into battle on behalf of Israel. It was Barak. Neither was she the "woman" chosen to gain the victory over Sisera. That honor was given to Jael. But Deborah is heralded as a champion in her own right. She wasn't seeking fame or attention for herself. She had a reputation of giving God the glory.

Deborah had two loves besides her husband: God and Israel. She had such a strong relationship with the Lord, that others knew and revered it. I think that was the reason that Barak wanted her present. She was so connected to God, it was like having the Lord himself present.

Deborah also loved Israel. The Bible says that she was a mother to them. Her loving and nurturing spirit wanted to relieve Israel from the pressure and bondage of Jabin. It had to break her heart to see the oppression of her people for 20 long years. So she did it for love. Her love for Israel yielded them peace. And she loved God. She made sure he got the praise. All attention went back to Him.

It was her close relationship with God and her heroic attitude that helped to secure the victory for Israel. And Israel had rest for 40 years.

Can God use you in an unconventional way? Just because it has never been done before doesn't mean that it shouldn't be done. Ten thousand men and 1 woman. Be bold. Be daring. Be that one woman who is willing to lead the men into battle. Step into the fight. Trust God and be fearless.

Deborah was a strong and courageous as a lioness. She led God's people back to Him, thereby insuring their freedom and victory.

BECOMING A FIERCE WOMAN

Do you have the heart of a lioness? How so or Why not?

_____

_____

_____

_____

Are people drawn to you because of your relationship with the Lord?   Yes   No   I don't know

Do others see you as a leader?
                 Yes   No   I don't know

Describe an act of leadership that demonstrates your fearlessness?

_____

_____

_____

_____

How can you grow as a leader?

_____

_____

_____

_____

What about Deborah's story stands out to you?

_____

_____

_____

_____

5
A STAR IS BORN:
FEARLESS ESTHER

Esther

Often we hear ministers speak negatively of Esther's hesitancy to step up to defend her nation. It is true. She was reluctant. Courage doesn't always appear clean and flawless. It is often torn and dirtied with episodes of fear. Nevertheless Esther, whose name means star, found her fortitude and stepped up as the heroine of Israel.

Israel had found itself in captivity by Persia. The enemy of Israel, the evil Haman, conspired to destroy the Hebrew people. Since Esther had replaced Vashti as queen, Mordecai (her uncle and adopted father) urged the young girl to go to the king on behalf of her people. She objected because she knew it was dangerous. She could possibly lose her life for going to the king without being summoned. He was already miffed behind the disrespect of Vashti. Caution wasn't unreasonable. Approaching the king was costly and she was just too afraid.

At Esther's resistance, Mordecai speaks sternly to her, "Don't think that you will escape in the king's house. If you do not speak up, God will send us help from another place. But you and yours will be destroyed. Have you considered that perhaps the position you hold is for such a time as this?"

Mordecai was urging the young queen to consider her purpose. Purpose is what moves us. This was exactly the reason that the Lord had placed Esther to be queen. It wasn't just for her to enjoy. It was for Israel.

Our positions, placement and favor is not just for us. God is moving us like pieces on a chess board. There is a master plan. And the Master is in charge. We should not resist God's urging. He is always operating by a plan. Sometimes we are privy to it, but many times we are not.

Esther's nationality had been hidden up until now. It was about to be uncovered, the Queen of Persia was a Jew. This was not by happenstance. Surely God was up to something.

Can you imagine being born to rescue a nation? It was Esther's divine assignment. To hold on to her life was pointless. We all will die, one day. No one will live forever on this earth. We are passing through. We are aliens to this land. We are here simply to do what we were born to do.

Mordecai's speech had been persuasive to the young queen. Esther responded with courage, "If I die, I die." She was now ready to march forward into danger. She let go of the outcome and surrendered her fear of death. God is in charge and if death is what it costs, then so be it.

Your response and mine must be "I was put here for this. It was for this hour that I was put into this world. We must proceed with the assignment, leaving the outcome up to God.

We know that Esther did not die for approaching the king. In fact, she had the king's favor. Because of it, she and her people were saved. And Haman was sentenced to the very persecution that he hoped to exact upon Israel. God had a secret weapon to use against the enemy. And that secret weapon was His star, Esther. Checkmate!

BECOMING A FIERCE WOMAN

What is your purpose on the earth?

_____

_____

_____

_____

Are you operating in it?   Yes   No

Do you find yourself fearful of doing what you were born to do?   Yes   No

Are you willing to die for your cause?
                              Yes   No

In what ways do you need to grow to complete your purpose on the earth?

_____

_____

_____

_____

What about Esther's story stands out to you?

_____

_____

_____

_____

_____

6
BRAVE :FEARLESS JAEL

Judges 4

It sounds like something straight out of a thriller. Sisera was running on foot. Israel was in hot pursuit. They had already defeated his army and they were coming to take him down. Out of breath, Sisera, the captain of King Jabin's army had come running with his tail tucked between his legs. Jael had been watching. She went out to meet him and convinced him to turn into her tent. Her husband was away, but she let him know that it was safe. "Don't be afraid", she conned him. He turned into her tent. He was exhausted and afraid.

The Kenite woman invited him in with the pretense of safety. He asked for a drink of water. She did him one better, she gave him milk and encouraged him to rest. And then without warning, after he had fallen asleep in the tent, the brutal murder ensued. Jael took the tent nails and hammered them right through his skull. The captain didn't even know what hit him. Just as it was prophesied, the enemy of Israel was dead by the hand of a woman. It was gruesome indeed. But this was war.

His blood must have splattered all over her hair, her clothes, her hands, and even in her face. This did not deter our protagonist. She didn't even rush to wash herself or change clothes. She rushed to tell Barak, that his nemesis was no longer alive. She showed him her kill.

It's interesting that Jael would do such a thing. There had been peace between Jabin, King of the Canaanites and the house of Heber, Jael's husband. So why did Jael execute such treachery upon her husband's ally? The Bible doesn't give us an answer. All we know is that what she did was the will of God. Her actions were both prophesied and praised. Sisera was not just the enemy of Israel, but he was the enemy of God.

This female warrior showed there was no weakness in her womanhood. She was a woman of strength. She would be considered in our time as a homemaker. So here we see Jael, as a homemaker by day and a warrior by night. She was willing to do what needed to be done. We contrast her moxie with that of Barak who didn't even want to go to battle without Deborah.

Jael was not timid or intimidated. She was courageous indeed! She is the second lioness who shows up to this particular battle.

When a lioness is hunting her prey, she works in concert with her sisters. The strategy often used is the ambush. One lioness is in pursuit and leads the prey into the path of the other. Her teammate waits for the perfect moment to spring an attack. This is the case with Jael and Deborah. The story of Deborah could not be told without Jael, the housewife or tent wife. We are not told if she has any type of leadership position. She was however the quiet lioness waiting for the ambush.

Sisera ran for safety straight into the tent of Jael. Two women warriors worked together to take down the enemy of Israel.

There are many great lessons we can pull from this

story. One is to be content where you are. God can use you in whatever season you are in. If you are a stay-at-home mom, be at peace. There is a kingdom work for you right in your home. Everybody can't be on the frontline. Be who you were created to be. You are important no matter where you are positioned.

Another lesson is that God wants us as women to work in harmony. We are not to be jealous or in competition with each other. He can use us all. He uses the stay-at-home mom right along with the Chairman of the Board. We are all on the same side, chasing the enemy of our souls.

BECOMING A FIERCE WOMAN

What life lesson can you pull out of this story?

_____
_____
_____
_____

Do you compare yourself to other women?

                  Yes   No

Are you content in the season that you are in?

                  Yes   No

Why or Why not?

_____
_____
_____
_____

What needs to happen to get to contentment?

_____
_____
_____
_____

What about Jael's story stands out to you?

_____
_____
_____
_____

7
THE GIFT: JOCHEBED

Exodus 2

The Hebrews multiplied at such an alarming rate that it put fear in the heart of Pharaoh. He was sure that their numbers and strength would cause them to overthrow his power. So he commanded that all newborn males be cast into the river to die. Drown the babies.

But one mother was intent on saving her baby boy's life. Jochebed was the mother of three. Miriam and Aaron were already of age and their lives were not in jeopardy. But this evil edict put her newborn at risk.

Jochebed cast her son onto the river and not into it. She carefully prepared a cradle to protect him and I am sure she prayed over him and then set him upon the Nile. She sent his sister to watch what would happen to him.

The daughter of Pharoah drew the baby out of the river and called him Moses. The Princess of Egypt knew that the baby was Hebrew and she was very much aware of her father's pronouncement upon the Jews. Unbeknownst to her, she was a key player in God's plan. The compassionate Princess brings the infant into her house to be raised as her own.

The Bible is silent about what Pharaoh had to say about

his daughter's new child. She hadn't been pregnant. Did he turn his head for the sake of his daughter or was he deceived in some way? We don't know. We do know that she became surrogate mother to Moses.

Miriam was sent by the royal maiden to fetch one of the Hebrew women to nurse the babe. Miriam brought her mother and his. This had to comfort Jochebed. She had protected her son by releasing him to God and now the Lord sent the baby right back to her. She was being paid to nurse her own son. God grants us favor in our obedience.

God had protected Moses. Her son would be safe, now. The Deliverer of Israel would be raised in Pharaoh's house right under his nose, by his own daughter. God had a funny way of doing things.

God had given Jochebed a small window with her son. She would be able to nurse him until he was weaned. From that time on, she would have to trust God to watch over him. This son she bore was not just for her own pleasure. He would bring deliverance to her people.

Moses was chosen by God. His life was purposed even before he was in Jochebed's womb. But before Moses was chosen, Jochebed was chosen. God needed a Jochebed who would risk her own life to save her son's. He needed a mother that would let go of her right to raise her son. God needed Jochebed's strength and faith. She was the perfect one to be mother to a deliverer.

She wouldn't be allowed to raise her son, kiss him, play with him or teach him Hebrew customs. She would have to watch him from afar. She would have to hear news of how he was doing. I'm sure there were days that her heart ached for her youngest child. How must it have felt to let another woman (and an Egyptian woman at that) have the pleasure of caring for her son? That had to be tough.

Selfless Jochebed was willing to give up her son so that his purpose could be fulfilled. He was a gift to Israel, and so was she. I'm sure she prayed countless hours for her babies. At the end, Jochebed's three children were reunited. They all served her God and worked together as leaders over Israel. What a legacy to leave on the earth! All three children in ministry together – a mother's dream!

Trusting God with our children is challenging at times. We are attached to them from the moment that they enter our wombs. We talk to them and sing to them before they are ever born. We are connected at the heart. And so when God says, "Let go. Give him/her to me", it doesn't feel easy. Especially when our eyes are on the child. The only way to truly let go is to put our eyes on the Lord. Look into the loving eyes of our Lord and open your grasp. Save my child, Lord. And He does just that and so much more.

BECOMING A FIERCE WOMAN

Do you trust God to take care of your child(ren)?

Yes   No

In what ways have you had to trust Him with your children?

_____
_____
_____
_____

What has been difficult to watch in the lives of your children?

_____
_____
_____
_____

What are your prayer targets for your children?

_____
_____
_____
_____

What about Jochebed's story stands out to you?

_____
_____
_____
_____

8
THE BEAUTY MARK: RAHAB

Joshua 2

In this passage, Joshua sends two spies to Jericho to spy out the land. Rahab, the harlot, receives the enemy spies and makes a decision to hide them instead of revealing them. That is rather curious for a foreigner and even more so for a prostitute. Why would she do such a thing? Why would she go to such lengths to deceive her own people and risk her life?

Verses 2:9-10 reads, "*⁹ And she said unto the men, I know that the LORD hath given you the land, and that your terror is fallen upon us, and that all the inhabitants of the land faint because of you.¹⁰ For we have heard how the LORD dried up the water of the Red sea for you, when ye came out of Egypt; and what ye did unto the two kings of the Amorites, that were on the other side Jordan, Sihon and Og, whom ye utterly destroyed.*

She had heard some things about these people, their God, and His power. The Lord's fame had spread abroad. He had destroyed 2 kings. The parting of the Red Sea had been a pretty big deal. Rahab believed the God of Israel to be the one true God. And not just her, but all the people of Jericho. She said they began to fear the moment they heard the report. In fact, her words were, *"neither did there remain any more courage in any man, because of you."* Wow! All the men were afraid. They lost courage because of Israel and Israel's God.

She bartered with the men not just for her life but the life of all her family: her parents and siblings, everyone that was connected to her.

This woman of the night, traded sides. She saw something in Israel's God that she didn't see in her own. She was willing to give everything up for this God she had heard so much about. Her decision yielded amazing results. She and her family were saved, and she also was grafted into the lineage of David and Jesus. Yes, the harlot.

Sometimes people are uncomfortable with those who have a checkered past, especially the type of past that she had. Sure we believe that all have sinned and fell short of God's glory, but somehow we still justify our sin as if it's not "that" bad. But in God's eyes, none of it is excusable.

Rahab had her sin tagged to her name. It's right out there for us all to read about. Even after she is redeemed and listed in the hall of faith in Hebrews chapter 11, she is still referred to as Rahab, the harlot. Why? David is not called, David, the adulterer. Moses is not called, Moses, the murderer. Is it because she is a woman and women received ill treatment. Or because she wasn't of Jewish descent? I doubt it. Did God leave it there to taunt her or remind her of her sin. That's not His character. I think it was part of her assignment, her ministry to us. I think God set it as her name forever to allow those of us with sin tags attached, to see He has made a way for us, too. We can be joined into the royal family. Rahab married Salmon, a prince in Israel and was made part of the royal ancestry of Jesus. Her son was Boaz. God reserved this special honor just for her. It's a beauty mark of sorts. Centuries of believers read her story and see a beauty they wouldn't otherwise see. Those who feel they can't be forgiven or those who don't understand the grace of God, can look to Rahab, the harlot, as a reminder of God's grace.

What does this mean to us? Rahab is a shadow of the Gentile church. Because she believed, she was engrafted into the family of God. Regardless of our spotted pasts, we can obtain salvation by faith. The Lord has a magnificent plan for our lives to adopt us and give us a godly inheritance.

There is more to you than meets the eye. So leave your shame behind. Just as Rahab helped secure the victory for Israel, God can use you for his glory as well. He came for sinners. So forget about your past. And look forward to a bright future...with your beauty mark – sin forgiven.

BECOMING A FIERCE WOMAN

Do you have sin in your past/present for which you are ashamed?

Yes   No

Do you believe you can be forgiven?

Yes   No

Why/Why not?

_____

_____

_____

_____

What is your beauty mark?

_____

_____

_____

_____

How can you use your beauty mark to give God glory?

_____

_____

_____

_____

What about Rahab's story stands out to you?

_____

_____

_____

_____

9
ADORED: MARY

Luke 1

"Be it unto me, according to thy Word" The angel had showed up on the scene and spoke to the young Mary of her future. She had been chosen to be the mother of God. What an honor! But coupled with that honor would be great affliction. She would have to lose in order to gain. But she responded with exhilaration and anticipation, "Be it unto me." Let it happen! I receive ALL that you have spoken!

WOW! What a statement of trust! Much was at stake. She had kept herself from worldliness. This young beauty had never known a man. There would be whispers about her being pregnant. Her honor would only be kept between her and God. Others would be left to think what they may.

Mary nobly accepted the challenge. She was not only obedient, she was willing. She didn't even know what her 'yes' would mean. Nevertheless, she offered it, anyway.

The cost was pretty high. Initially, she was rejected by her fiancé, Joseph. He sought to divorce her. That had to hurt. The man she was to marry, no longer wanted her, all because she said yes to God. (The angel of God corrected him in a dream. But it still had to sting).

She was saying yes to labor in a barn full of stinky, noisy animals? Would she doubt God's plan? Would she accuse and blame Joseph that he couldn't do better? "It's your fault Joseph that you can't take better care of me?" She didn't. Even as a young girl, she knew that her steps were ordered by God. So she didn't lay this charge at Joseph's feet.

Mary didn't have the first clue to what she was saying yes to, but she certainly knew to whom. And that's what made the difference. There were still many more challenges that lay ahead. She would continuously meditate on the things that had been prophesied to her.

She became a part of her son's ministry. She travelled with him. She stayed right there beside him, cheering him on.

The most difficult challenge of this honor would be watching Him die. He was her Savior and her Son. Neither role was more difficult than the other. He had come to save the world from their sins and in return they would openly mock, beat, and crucify him. This would be the thanks He would receive for all the healings, deliverances, and miracles. There would be no appreciation for his love and His service. He was sentenced to death on a cross. Her heart would be broken.

As painful and traumatic as this was, Mary had signed up for it all. She had said yes. "Be it unto me, according to your word." She was essentially saying, "let whatever happen that You will to happen. Let your word unfold in my life." She was willing to do whatever God required of her. While she may have been taken aback, God wasn't. Strangely enough, every trial, every slur, every slight was part of His great plan. Mary knew it. And she trusted God through it all. That didn't mean she wouldn't feel the pain or shed many tears. On the contrary, she would. Nevertheless she submitted to God a great big fat sloppy, Yes!

She was the girl who trusted God. Thirty three years later, she was the woman who continued to trust Him. Though years passed and she changed, her reliance on God did not. It only grew stronger. She adored her God and He adored her. And the Lord gifted John with the honor of caring for her. God didn't leave her empty, "John will be your son and you will be his mother".

Do you trust Him? Are you willing to say yes to an unrevealed future? Do you trust God enough to lose in order to gain? Be brave enough to say, "Be it unto me according to your word."

BECOMING A FIERCE WOMAN

How much do you love God?

_____

Are you willing to say yes to an unrevealed future no matter what the cost?

Yes   No

What uncertainty are you facing today?

_____
_____
_____
_____

Is it possible that this is part of God's plan?

Yes   No

Do you blame others for uncomfortable situations in your life?

Yes   No

Why? Why not?

_____
_____
_____
_____

What about Mary's story stands out to you?

_____
_____
_____
_____

10
LOVE STORY: FEARLESS RUTH

Ruth

A young woman fell in love and her life changed forever. Her name is Ruth. She was the grandmother of King David. How did this foreigner wiggle her way into the family tree of Jesus?

This young widow found herself in a precarious situation. The men of the family were all dead. Not only had her husband died, but so had her brother-in-law and father-in-law. She was left alone with her sister-in-law and mother-in-law to figure things out. Times were tough and a famine held Moab captive.

Naomi instructed her 2 daughters in law, to go home to their families because she had nothing left for them. Orpah conceded, but Ruth contested. She had found love and she wasn't willing to walk away from it. Ruth denounced her own life to hang on to Naomi's. Her words were compelling, They dripped with loyalty and fierce adoration. "Your people shall be my people. And your God my own. I will go wherever you go."

Ruth had found purpose in love. Her connection to Naomi would forever alter her life. It was destined by God that this young girl would be the travel companion to Naomi in her grief. He would use Naomi to unleash the destiny of this young woman. And He would use Ruth to change the course of history for the older woman. It was by divine providence. The two shared a history and a family. And now they were only connected by God....or love.

Mothers-in-law and daughters-in-law often find themselves in contentious relationships. However, this was not the case of Ruth and Naomi. This story spotlights the character of Naomi. She had to be an amazing woman. Her daughters-in-law adored her and wanted to be with her. Even Orpah only returned home after Naomi's urging. The two girls loved her immensely.

Ruth could have rightfully chosen to go home to her family as Orpah had done. But she was too connected. Too much love had been lavished upon her. She no longer worshiped the gods of her people. She had been awakened to a new relationship with Naomi's God. She was different. She couldn't go back. Home was wherever Naomi was.

Naomi was grief-stricken and bitter. She probably wasn't that great of a traveling companion. She felt her God had turned against her. But as negative as she was, Ruth stuck by her. She didn't religiously toss Naomi aside because she wasn't saying the "right" things. Nor did she scold her for her accusation against God. Ruth's compassion kept her close to Naomi. She hurt for her. And this was her opportunity to be there for the mother who had been there for her these 10 years.

The two women were poor and broken. When they arrived in Bethlehem, it was harvest season. Ruth jumped in and begin attending to the needs of her mother-in-law with unfailing devotion. She went to work to gather food for the two of them.

When Naomi discovered that Ruth was gleaning in a

family member's field, she gave Ruth strategic wisdom. She was positioning the young widow for destiny. And Ruth followed Naomi's instruction without objections and without questioning. She trusted her fully.

As a result, Ruth found favor with Boaz. He took to her and instructed his servants to give her extra food. He wasn't opposed to being in relationship with this stranger. His dad had done the same thing when he married Boaz's mother, Rahab. (You remember the lady with the beauty mark).

Boaz later redeemed the young woman and made her his wife. The blessing laid upon Ruth's head. She would finally give birth to a son. His name was Obed, (he was the grandfather of King David). All because she fell in love with Naomi and Naomi's God.

"For your daughter-in-law is better to thee than 7 sons", this was the praise the other women raved to Naomi. Wow! What a testament to the love Ruth had for her mother-in-law! Having 1 son was considered an honor. But to be better than 7 sons – WOW! Ruth was a great lover. Her love and kindness never failed.

It's interesting that Ruth was still considered Naomi's daughter-in-law. Isn't that odd? Ruth's husband was dead and Ruth didn't have any children by Naomi's son. In fact, she was now remarried to Boaz who was not Naomi's son. And she was still called Naomi's daughter-in-law. What must have it been like to have 2 mothers-in- law? Ruth was daughter-in-law to both Rahab and Naomi. She was the best one for the job.

Our family are not just those connected by blood but those who love our God. Ruth was a selfless woman. Ruth fell in love with God and the new mother He assigned her. And she returned the lavish love that she received. Jesus challenges us all when he says who is my family... but those who obey the Word. Ruth accepted the challenge and it changed her world.

BECOMING A FIERCE WOMAN

Is there someone who loves you as if you were their own blood?   Yes   No

Is there someone you love like that who is not your own kin?   Yes   No

Do you have a good relationship with your mother?
                                                       Yes   No

Do you have a good relationship with your mother-in-law?
                                                       Yes   No

What can you do to improve either of those relationships?

_____

_____

_____

_____

Identify the person that God has brought into your life to mentor/disciple you?

_____

Are you handling that relationship in the way that pleases God?   Yes   No

What about Ruth's story stands out to you?

_____

_____

_____

_____

11
DREAM GIRLS: FEARLESS DAUGHTERS OF ZELOPHEHAD

Numbers 27

Zelophehad had no sons. He had five children, but not one boy in the lot. These five young girls, Mahlah, Noah, Hoglah, Milcah, and Tirzah were left to speak for themselves after their father had died.

Moses had gathered together the tribes for a census and to distribute the land. According to the law, the girls were not entitled to anything. The law was set to keep the possessions in families and so it was given to the sons to preserve the father's name and legacy. Zelophehad's girls were young and had not yet married. So according to the law, they would be left with nothing.

They had spent time discussing this situation among themselves. They would be cut out of their dad's inheritance by default – simply because they were born female. It just didn't seem fair. They did not believe that this was consistent with the nature of the God they served. They dreamed that if they could approach the council, perhaps things would change. Something needed to be done. They were compelled to take action.

Though they were young, they weren't weak women. They did not resolve to just sit and pout it out. Nor were they the type to say, "It must be God's will" and just let it be. And they certainly weren't going to act unseemly by throwing a hissy fit. They decided that they needed to challenge the law.

These were wise sisters. They mustered up their courage and went to the tent of meetings, together. They didn't send a representative, but they all went. They showed their unity and their strength. The Fab 5 stood in agreement as they appealed to Moses, Eleazar the priest, the princes, and all the congregation. The girls spoke with humility, "Our father was not involved in Korah's rebellion. He died in the wilderness in his own sin." The question they presented to all who were gathered, "Why should our father's name die out simply because he had no son?"

It was a good question. God determined who would be born to whom, not man. So should Zelophehad be punished because he could not bear a son? It is certain that he wanted a son. For in that time and culture, it was natural for men to want sons. However, it had not happened for him. Was he to be punished for what God allowed or didn't allow? Even Moses did not know how to answer these ladies. So Moses in his wisdom. took the matter to God.

God spoke, "These daughters are correct. You absolutely must give them their father's inheritance". Wait. What?! Yes, the law was changed just like that. There was no ritual or sacrifice required. No waiting period. God not only gave the girls their petition, but the law was changed permanently to include all daughters who found themselves in this situation.

After Moses was dead and Joshua was in charge, the daughters brought up the matter to Joshua who was in charge, Eleazar, and the princes, reminding them of what

God said to Moses. Joshua honored their request and the daughters received a double portion because their father was the first born son. (Joshua 17) They went from receiving nothing to getting a double portion because they defied tradition. What if they had left the matter alone? They didn't and God rewarded them for their fearlessness.

Why wasn't this a part of the law in the beginning? The God who knows all things had left this part out of the law. Why? I venture to say, to provoke His daughters to approach him. He often asks us to prove Him. He wants us to understand that we work in concert with Him. There are some things left up to mankind to execute. God is not going to do everything for us. Sometimes we have to ask for what is ours. We must gather our courage and point out what is missing. God wants us to speak up and stand up for what is right. Especially in their male dominated culture, God wanted those daughters to know they could be heard. Yes, God does hear the petitions of women.

What is it that God is trying to provoke you to do? To say? Is there a cause that you need to plead? Is there something lacking in your life or some injustice that seems to have no answer? The Lord may be provoking you. You may be the catalyst for change. Consider that for a moment.

What these girls did was unprecedented. Because the sisters were brave enough to approach those who handled the law, this changed the future for generations of women.

Don't just accept your circumstance. Move forward in faith. God is able to bring forth change.
Numbers 26, 36, 37

There is neither Jew nor Greek, slave nor free, male nor female, for you are all one in Christ Jesus. If you belong to Christ, then you are Abraham's seed, and heirs according to the promise."

BECOMING A FIERCE WOMAN

Is there some situation that you or someone you love is/are facing that seems unjust?

Yes   No

If yes, what is it?

_____
_____
_____
_____

Have you just accepted it?   Yes   No

Are you afraid of rejection?   Yes   No

Is the Lord nudging to step up and fight?

Yes   No

What can you do to rally for yourself or others?

_____
_____
_____
_____

What about the Daughters of Zelophehad's story stands out to you?

_____
_____
_____
_____

12
FEARLESS YOU?

The women featured in the preceding chapters are normal everyday women who were submitted to a supernatural and all-powerful God. They were prodded, drawn in, provoked, and captivated by God to do the amazing things they did. They took a deep breath and decided to trust God. That's how you show your brave. Courage equals unwavering trust in God. And because they did, they were highlighted in scripture. Because they loved Him and embraced their calls, their stories were shared.

It is time that you share your story. There is something quite special and extraordinary about you. The common trait that the others profiled in this book share is their sheer trust. If you can trust God, you will do great feats. He will use you to impact your family, community, and/or nation.

There is and never will be another person just like you. You are custom designed by the Great Creator, fearfully and wonderfully crafted. You are his royal priesthood, his chosen vessel, God's masterpiece. You are his precious jewel. It doesn't matter if others agree. God has said it. Therefore it is so.

He thinks about you more than any other lover. Psalm 139:17-18 says it like this, How precious also are thy thoughts unto me, O God! How great is the sum of them. If I should count them, they are more in number than the sand: when I awake, I am still with thee.

If you can number the sand, then you count his thoughts about you. Can you imagine anyone thinking of you that much?! He loves you so much that He opened up His arms wide and died for you. You can trust a love like that.

Before you ever entered your mother's womb, God thought about what gifts, talents and abilities that you would need to complete your assignment. He equipped you with all of them. He also preplanned what time in history that you would come to earth and for how long. And you are here, now.

This is your set time. Do what you were born to do. God is waiting for you to live out your adventure. The prerequisite is simple trust. It's the only way to a fearless life.

It doesn't matter how you started out or what family you were born into. Forget about the mistakes and poor choices you've made in the past. Just know that there is a God who loves and adores you. You are the apple of His eye. And you were chosen by Him to make a difference in the earth. Go live out your story. Be fierce. Be fabulous. Be fearless! You were born for this!

Write your story: Who are you? Who did God create you to be? What did He intend for you to do? What gifts, abilities, and talents did He lend to you? How have you offered them back to Him?

_____

_____

_____

ABOUT THE AUTHOR

Crystal Jones is a fearless daughter of God. She is the devoted wife and ministry partner of Apostle Oscar Jones. They have been married for more than 36 years. Together, the couple celebrate their 7 awesome adult children and 8 amazing grandchildren. Crystal leads the Fearless Women's Conference which travels nationwide. She loves women's ministry and mentors young women all over country. She also has a heart for marriages and family ministry (Marriage For A Lifetime Ministries) which she labors in with her husband. Crystal is living her own adventure from her home base near Atlanta, GA.

Other Books By the Author

Fearless A 31 Day Devotional
I Want A Husband, Too
No Longer A Dream: A Step by Step Guide to Writing Your 1st Book
Not Without My Daughters (Mentoring Handbook)
The S Word: What Submission Is Not
Unafraid

Books Co-authored

A Woman's Place Leading Ladies Anthology
Church Unusual by Oscar & Crystal Jones
Extreme Money Makeover by Oscar & Crystal Jones
Fast Food for the Married Soul by Oscar & Crystal Jones
Hot Dates for Married Lovers by Oscar & Crystal Jones
Leadershift by Oscar & Crystal Jones
Let the Prophets Speak by Torrona Tillman & Crystal Jones
Naked Sex by Oscar & Crystal Jones
Ring Talks by Oscar & Crystal Jones
The Newlywed Handbook by Oscar & Crystal Jones
When the Vow Breaks by Oscar & Crystal Jones

www.ingramcontent.com/pod-product-compliance
Lightning Source LLC
Chambersburg PA
CBHW070029110426
42741CB00034B/2692